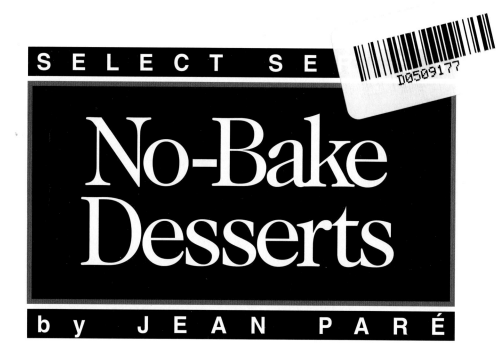

SELECT SE

No-Bake Desserts

by JEAN PARÉ

selected recipes from

COOKBOOKS

No-Bake Desserts

First printing February 1998

Canadian Cataloguing in Publication Data
Paré, Jean
　　　No-bake desserts

Includes index.
Published also in French under title: Desserts sans cuisson.
ISBN 1-896891-24-1

　　　1. Desserts. 2. Cookery (Cold dishes).
I. Title.

TX773.P3598 1998　　　641.8'6 C97-900798-4

Published simultaneously in Canada and the United States of America by **The Recipe Factory Inc.** in conjunction with **Company's Coming Publishing Limited** 2311 - 96 Street Edmonton, Alberta, Canada　T6N 1G3 Tel:　403 • 450-6223 Fax:　403 • 450-1857

No-Bake Desserts was created thanks to the dedicated efforts of the people and organizations listed below.

COMPANY'S COMING PUBLISHING LIMITED

Author	Jean Paré
President	Grant Lovig
V.P., Product Development	Kathy Knowles
Production Coordinator	Derrick Sorochan
Design	Nora Cserny
Typesetting	Marlene Crosbie
	Jaclyn Draker

THE RECIPE FACTORY INC.

Research & Development Manager	Nora Prokop
Test Kitchen Supervisor	Lynda Elsenheimer
Editor/Food Stylist	Stephanie With
Assistant Editor	Michelle White
Photographer	Stephe Tate Photo
Prop Stylist	Gabriele McEleney

Our special thanks to the following businesses for providing extensive props for photography.

Chintz & Company
Creations By Design
Eaton's
Enchanted Kitchen
La Cache
Le Gnome
Scona Clayworks
Sears Canada
Stokes
The Bay

Color separations, printing, and binding by Friesens, Altona, Manitoba, Canada
Printed in Canada

FRONT COVER
Clockwise from top right:
Black Forest Soufflé, page 76
Lime Chiffon Pie, page 51
Peanut Squares, page 67
TV Roll, page 62
Apricots Romanoff, page 41
Cherry Chocolate Squares, page 66
Lemon Chiffon Cheesecake, page 16

Table of Contents

The Jean Paré Story

Jean Paré grew up understanding that the combination of family, friends and home cooking is the essence of a good life. From her mother she learned to appreciate good cooking, while her father praised even her earliest attempts. When she left home she took with her many acquired family recipes, her love of cooking and her intriguing desire to read recipe books like novels!

In 1963, when her four children had all reached school age, Jean volunteered to cater to the 50th anniversary of the Vermilion School of Agriculture, now Lakeland College. Working out of her home, Jean prepared a dinner for over 1000 people which launched a flourishing catering operation that continued for over eighteen years. During that time she was provided with countless opportunities to test new ideas with immediate feedback—resulting in empty plates and contented customers! Whether preparing cocktail sandwiches for a house party or serving a hot meal for 1500 people, Jean Paré earned a reputation for good food, courteous service and reasonable prices.

"Why don't you write a cookbook?" Time and again, as requests for her recipes mounted, Jean was asked that question. Jean's response was to team up with her son, Grant Lovig, in the fall of 1980 to form Company's Coming Publishing Limited. April 14, 1981, marked the debut of "150 DELICIOUS SQUARES", the first Company's Coming cookbook in what soon would become Canada's most popular cookbook series. By 1995, sales had surpassed ten million cookbooks.

Jean Paré's operation has grown from the early days of working out of a spare bedroom in her home to operating a large and fully equipped test kitchen in Vermilion, Alberta, near the home she and her husband Larry built. Full-time staff has grown steadily to include marketing personnel located in major cities across Canada plus selected U.S. markets. Home Office is located in Edmonton, Alberta, where distribution, accounting and administration functions are headquartered in the company's own 20,000 square foot facility. Growth continues with the recent addition of the Recipe Factory, a 2700 square foot test kitchen and photography studio located in Edmonton.

Company's Coming cookbooks are now distributed throughout Canada and the United States plus numerous overseas markets, all under the guidance of Jean's daughter, Gail Lovig. The series is published in English and French, plus a Spanish language edition is available in Mexico. Familiar and trusted Company's Coming-style recipes are now available in a variety of formats in addition to the bestselling soft cover series.

Jean Paré's approach to cooking has always called for quick and easy recipes using everyday ingredients. She continues to gain new supporters by adhering to what she calls "the golden rule of cooking": never share a recipe you wouldn't use yourself. It's an approach that works—*ten million times over!*

Foreword

On a hot summer day, the last thing you want to do is turn on the oven. Instead, turn to the pages of *No-Bake Desserts* and pick a recipe—you won't need your oven for any one of them. Whether you find yourself at the cottage with just a hot plate, or suddenly inconvenienced at home by an oven that refuses to work, it's still possible to create a delicious and tempting dessert.

Some of these recipes call for simple stovetop preparation and are so easy to assemble—like Choco-Ginger Cookies—that they are ready to be enjoyed right away. A microwave is a handy alternative to your stove when melting or boiling is called for. Other recipes may require refrigeration or freezing; read through the complete recipe before you start and note if chilling or freezing time is necessary.

For added convenience, pre-baked pie shells have been recommended for preparing any of the dessert pies in this book. You can either bake and freeze your own pie crusts or keep commercial graham or chocolate crumb crusts on hand.

The best feature of all is that these great recipes allow you the opportunity get other tasks done—no need to linger around a hot kitchen to watch your dessert bake!

Refresh your taste buds with a chilled dessert such as Danish Cream Squares, or warm your spirits with Chocolate Cream Pudding or Blueberry Sauce over Crêpes. White Chocolate Mousse is certain to be enjoyed by everyone at your next dinner party, or when company arrives for coffee and dessert.

Be it a hot summer day or a cold stormy night, *No-Bake Desserts* will always be your convenient, time-saving guide to a world of delicious, sweet treats.

Blueberry-Sauced Crêpes, page 42.
Chocolate-Sauced Crêpes, page 42.

It is so easy to elaborate on a simple cake by filling it with fruit, pudding, custard or pie filling to make a cake-type dessert. All of these recipes contain an already-made chocolate, white, angel food, sponge or pound cake. Very convenient when you have guests coming for dessert.

TUNNEL OF PEACHES

A light, tasty and pretty dessert.

Baked angel food cake	1	1
Vanilla pudding and pie filling, 4 serving size	1	1
Milk	2 cups	500 mL
Whipping cream (or 1 envelope topping)	1 cup	250 mL
Almond flavoring	½ tsp.	2 mL
Canned sliced peaches, drained	14 oz.	398 mL
Whipping cream (or 1 envelope topping, optional)	1 cup	250 mL

Cut a 1 inch (2.5 cm) thick layer from top of cake. Set aside. Hollow out cake leaving inside and outside walls, as well as a 1 inch (2.5 cm) thickness at the bottom. Cut removed cake into small chunks. Set aside.

Cook pudding and milk according to directions on package. Chill thoroughly.

Whip cream and almond flavoring until stiff. Fold into cooled pudding. Add removed cake chunks and sliced peaches. Fold in. Spoon into tunnel. Place removed layer on top. May be iced with additional whipped cream, or may be served plain. Makes 16 slices.

Pictured on page 9.

ZUCCOTTO

Such an elegant dessert! A chocolate cake mold filled with a combination of chocolate, cherries and cream. Easier to make than it looks.

Baked chocolate cake layer, 9 inch (22 cm)	1	1
Prepared orange juice	¼ cup	60 mL
Brandy flavoring	¼ tsp.	1 mL
Whipping cream (or 1 envelope topping)	1 cup	250 mL
Icing (confectioner's) sugar	2 tbsp.	30 mL
Toasted hazelnuts	¼ cup	60 mL
Canned pitted cherries, drained and halved (or fresh)	½ cup	125 mL
Semisweet chocolate baking squares, grated	2 × 1 oz.	2 × 28 g

Cut cake into 2 layers. Choose an 8 cup (2 L) gently rounded bowl. Ease 1 layer inside of bowl, pushing down to form a shell. If it breaks, fit in as best you can. Mix orange juice and brandy flavoring. Sprinkle over shell.

Whip cream and icing sugar together until stiff.

Fold in nuts, cherries and chocolate. Spoon into cake shell. If top of mold is smaller than second cake layer (it should be about 7¼ inches, 18 cm) trim to fit. Place over cream mixture. Chill for at least 4 hours. Unmold onto serving plate. Slices into 6 or 8 wedges.

Pictured on page 9.

PARTY DESSERT PIE

A perfectly light dessert after a heavy meal. Best eaten fresh.

Baked angel food cake	½	½
Envelope unflavored gelatin	1 × ¼ oz.	1 × 7 g
Water	¼ cup	60 mL
Granulated sugar	½ cup	125 mL
Egg yolks (large)	4	4
Milk	½ cup	125 mL
Unsweetened chocolate baking square, cut up	1 × 1 oz.	1 × 28 g
Egg whites (large), room temperature	4	4
Granulated sugar	¼ cup	60 mL
Vanilla	1 tsp.	5 mL

Cut the ½ angel food cake into 3 layers, then cut or break into ¾ to 1 inch (2 to 2.5 cm) cubes into large bowl. Cover.

Sprinkle gelatin over water in small dish. Let stand.

Stir first amount of sugar and egg yolks together in top of double boiler. Stir in milk. Add chocolate. Cook, stirring often, until smooth and thickened. Add gelatin mixture. Stir to dissolve. Chill until mixture starts to thicken, stirring and scraping down sides every 5 minutes.

Beat egg whites in medium bowl until soft peaks form. Continue beating, as you gradually add second amount of sugar, until stiff. Stir in vanilla. Fold in chocolate mixture. Pour over cake in bowl. Gently fold until all pieces of cake are coated. Pour into greased 10 inch (25 cm) pie plate. Chill for about 3 hours. Serves 6 to 8.

Top: Tunnel Of Peaches, page 6. Middle: Zuccotto, page 7.
Bottom: Cherry Banana Slice, page 19.

APRICOT TRIFLE

A very good and very different trifle.

Pound cake, sliced (or lady fingers)	1	1
Canned apricots, drained, juice reserved	2 x 14 oz.	2 x 398 mL
Reserved apricot juice	⅓ cup	75 mL
Sherry (or alcohol-free sherry)	¼ cup	60 mL
Custard powder	¼ cup	60 mL
Milk	2½ cups	625 mL
Granulated sugar	3 tbsp.	50 mL
Almond flavoring	½ tsp.	2 mL
Grated orange peel	2 tsp.	10 mL
Raisins	1 tbsp.	15 mL
Toasted slivered almonds	1 tbsp.	15 mL
TOPPING		
Whipping cream (or ½ envelope topping)	½ cup	125 mL
Granulated sugar	1 tsp.	5 mL
Vanilla	¼ tsp.	1 mL
Raisins	2 tsp.	10 mL
Toasted slivered almonds	2 tsp.	10 mL

Line sides of glass bowl, about 2 quart (2 L) size, with cake slices about ¼ inch (6 cm) thick.

Reserve 8 apricot halves for topping.

Mix apricot juice and sherry. Drizzle over pound cake.

Measure custard powder into 4 cup (1 L) measuring cup. Add a little milk. Stir until smooth. Add remaining milk, sugar, almond flavoring, orange peel, raisins and almonds. Stir. Microwave, uncovered, on high (100%) power for about 5 minutes. Stir. Microwave on high (100%) power for about 2 minutes until mixture thickens. Cool. Gently stir in apricots. Pour over pound cake in bowl. Chill.

(continued on next page)

Topping: Whip cream, sugar and vanilla together in small bowl until stiff. Spread over trifle.

Arrange reserved apricots over top. Sprinkle with raisins and almonds. Serves 8.

Pictured below.

TRIFLE IN A PAN

Here is a way to make a moist trifle and know exactly how many servings it will provide. Simple to make and store.

White cake layer, baked in 9 × 9 inch (22 × 22 cm) pan	1	1
Sherry, sprinkle (or fruit juice)		
Raspberry jam	½ cup	125 mL
Vanilla pudding and pie filling, 4 serving size	1	1
Milk	2 cups	500 mL
Envelope dessert topping, prepared	1	1

Sprinkle cake with sherry and let soak in. Spread with raspberry jam.

Cook pudding with milk according to directions on package. Cool thoroughly. Spread over jam layer.

Cover with topping. Chill until ready to use. Cuts into 9 generous pieces.

Left: Apricot Trifle, page 10.
Right: Sherry Trifle, page 12.

SHERRY TRIFLE

A grand finale to a meal.

Sponge or pound cake	1	1
Raspberry jam or other red jam	⅓ cup	75 mL
Sherry (or alcohol-free sherry)	⅓ cup	75 mL
CUSTARD		
Milk	3 cups	750 mL
Custard powder	3 tbsp.	50 mL
Granulated sugar	6 tbsp.	100 mL
Salt, scant measure	¾ tsp.	4 mL
Vanilla	2 tbsp.	30 mL
Large eggs	2	2
TOPPING		
Whipping cream	1 cup	250 mL
Granulated sugar	1 tbsp.	15 mL
Vanilla	1 tsp.	5 mL
Almonds, halved or slivered	2 tbsp.	30 mL
Maraschino cherries	11	11

Cut cake to make 10 slices approximately the size of a deck of cards. Spread 5 slices with jam. Press the other 5 slices over jam. Cut each sandwich into cubes. Place cubes into pretty glass bowl. Sprinkle sherry over cake. Let stand to absorb.

Custard: Heat milk in heavy saucepan until boiling.

Combine custard powder, sugar and salt in small bowl. Stir to mix thoroughly. Add vanilla and eggs. Mix. Stir into boiling milk until thickened slightly. Remove from heat and cool a few minutes. While still quite warm pour over cake. Cover with foil. Chill. Foil will prevent a crust from forming.

Topping: Whip cream, sugar and vanilla together until stiff. Spread over chilled custard.

Decorate top with almonds and cherries. Place 8 cherries around outside edge and 3 in center. Serves 8.

Pictured on page 11.

·P A R É
pointer

He wanted the

doctor to treat him

but he had to pay

just like the rest of us.

LEMON-FILLED CAKE

A lovely lemon-layered loaf cake with very thin layers of cake. A light and refreshing end to a lunch.

Lemon pudding and pie filling, 4 serving size	1	1
Egg yolks (large)	2	2
Egg whites (large), room temperature	2	2
Pound cake, part or all	1	1
Whipping cream (or 1 envelope topping)	1 cup	250 mL
Granulated sugar	2 tsp.	10 mL
Vanilla	½ tsp.	2 mL

Prepare lemon filling using 2 egg yolks according to directions on package. Remove from heat.

Beat egg whites in small bowl until stiff. Fold into hot filling.

Cut cake into ⅓ to ½ inch (8 to 12 mm) thick slices. Line 9 x 5 x 3 inch (22 x 12 x 7 cm) loaf pan with foil. Layer as follows, then chill:

1. Cake slices

2. ½ lemon filling

3. Cake slices

4. ½ lemon filling

5. Cake slices

Whip cream, sugar and vanilla together in small bowl until stiff. Serve pieces topped with whipped cream, or cover top sides of each piece, or frost whole loaf before cutting. Serves 6.

Pictured on this page.

BOSTON CREAM PIE

It's a piece of cake!

Baked white cake layers, 8 inch (20 cm)	2	2
FILLING		
Milk	1 cup	250 mL
All-purpose flour	¼ cup	60 mL
Granulated sugar	¼ cup	60 mL
Large egg	1	1
Vanilla	½ tsp.	2 mL
GLAZE		
Icing (confectioner's) sugar	1 cup	250 mL
Cocoa	2 tbsp.	30 mL
Butter or hard margarine, melted	1 tbsp.	15 mL
Water or milk	4 tsp.	20 mL

Whipped cream, for garnish

Both cake layers may be used, or, if preferred, slice 1 layer to make 2 layers out of it.

Filling: Heat milk in heavy saucepan on medium until boiling.

Measure flour and sugar into small bowl. Stir thoroughly. Stir in egg and vanilla. Pour into hot milk, stirring, while mixture boils and thickens. Cool well.

Glaze: Beat all 4 ingredients together, adding a bit more liquid if necessary to make a barely pourable glaze.

To assemble, spread custard between layers. Spread glaze over top only. If you like, allow a bit to dribble over sides. Serve with or without whipped cream. Chill for at least 1 hour before serving. Serves 12.

TIP

If you have a pound cake that's been in the freezer for a long time or find a special sale on day-old or stale plain cakes, use them in these recipes. The added moisture of the puddings or fillings "bring them back to life".

These delicate cheesecakes are a wonder because they do not have to be baked. Chilled cheesecakes are generally lighter in texture than baked cheesecakes. This is ideal for hot summer days when you do not want to turn the oven on. Very refreshing.

COOL RASPBERRY

Can be used as an opener for lunch or as dessert.

FIRST LAYER		
Cooking apples, peeled, cored and sliced (such as McIntosh)	3	3
Water	1 cup	250 mL
Raspberry-flavored gelatin (jelly powder)	1 × 3 oz.	1 × 85 g
Frozen raspberries, in heavy syrup, partially thawed	10 oz.	284g
SECOND LAYER		
Whipping cream (or 1 envelope topping)	1 cup	250 mL
Cream cheese, softened	4 oz.	125 g
Granulated sugar	2 tbsp.	30 mL
Vanilla	1 tsp.	5 mL

First Layer: Cook apples in water until soft. Add gelatin. Stir to dissolve.

Add raspberries with syrup. Stir until completely thawed. Pour into 8 x 8 inch (20 x 20 cm) pan. Chill until firm.

Second Layer: Whip cream until stiff. Set aside.

Using same beaters, beat cream cheese, sugar and vanilla together until smooth and light. Fold into whipped cream. Spread over gelatin. Chill. Cuts into 9 squares.

LEMON CHIFFON CHEESECAKE

A frothy delicate delight both to the eye and the palate. A no-bake wonder.

CRUST

Butter or hard margarine	¼ cup	60 mL
Graham cracker crumbs	1¼ cups	300 mL
Granulated sugar	2 tbsp.	30 mL

FILLING

Envelopes unflavored gelatin	2 x ¼ oz.	2 x 7 g
Cold water	½ cup	125 mL
Egg yolks (large)	2	2
Milk	½ cup	125 mL
Granulated sugar	1 cup	250 mL
Salt	1 tsp.	5 mL
Creamed cottage cheese, blender smoothed (or sieved)	2 cups	500 mL
Grated peel and juice of 1 lemon		
Lemon juice, fresh or bottled	2 tbsp.	30 mL
Vanilla	1 tsp.	5 mL
Egg whites (large), room temperature	2	2
Whipping cream (or 1 envelope topping)	1 cup	250 mL

Crust: Melt butter in saucepan. Add graham crumbs and sugar. Stir to mix. Pack into bottom and up sides of ungreased 9 inch (22 cm) springform or 8 x 8 inch (20 x 20 cm) pan. Chill.

Filling: Sprinkle gelatin over water in top of double boiler. Let stand for 5 minutes. Place over boiling water.

Add yolks and beat with spoon. Stir in milk, sugar and salt. Heat and stir over hot water until gelatin and sugar are dissolved. Chill until syrupy.

Fold cottage cheese, peel, lemon juice and vanilla into thickened gelatin.

Beat egg whites until stiff. Using same beaters, whip cream until stiff. Fold egg whites into gelatin mixture, then fold in whipped cream. Pour over crust. Chill. Serves 12.

Pictured on front cover.

P A R É
pointer

And where else do

old Volkswagens go

but to the old Volk's

home.

PEACHES AND CREAM

Fluffy and creamy. The cream cheese in the topping gives a distinctive flavor.

CRUST

Butter or hard margarine	**½ cup**	**125 mL**
Graham cracker crumbs	**2 cups**	**500 mL**
Brown sugar, packed	**⅓ cup**	**75 mL**

FILLING

Canned sliced peaches, drained, juice reserved	**2 x 14 oz.**	**2 x 398 mL**
Reserved juice, plus water to make	**2 cups**	**500 mL**
Granulated sugar	**¼ cup**	**60 mL**
Cornstarch	**¼ cup**	**60 mL**
Cream cheese, softened	**8 oz.**	**250 g**
Granulated sugar	**1 cup**	**250 mL**
Whipping cream (or 2 envelopes topping)	**2 cups**	**500 mL**

Crust: Melt butter in saucepan. Stir in graham crumbs and brown sugar. Reserve ½ cup (125 mL) and press remaining crumbs in ungreased 9 x 13 inch (22 x 33 cm) pan.

Filling: Combine peaches, juice with water, sugar and cornstarch in saucepan. Heat and stir until mixture boils and thickens. Cool.

Beat cream cheese with sugar until light and fluffy. Whip cream until stiff. Fold into cheese mixture. Spread ½ on prepared crust. Spoon thickened peaches over top. Spoon second ½ cheese mixture over as best you can. Sprinkle with reserved crumbs. Chill. Cuts into 15 pieces.

Pictured on this page.

CURAÇAO CHEESECAKE

This KER-a-sow cheesecake is very delicate. Flavor is excellent.

CRUST		
Butter or hard margarine	⅓ cup	75 mL
Graham cracker crumbs	1¼ cups	300 mL
Brown sugar	2 tbsp.	30 mL
FILLING		
Envelopes unflavored gelatin	2 × ¼ oz.	2 × 7 g
Water	⅓ cup	75 mL
Cream cheese, softened	8 oz.	250 g
Creamed cottage cheese	1 cup	250 mL
Sour cream	½ cup	125 mL
Granulated sugar	½ cup	125 mL
Grated peel and juice of 1 orange		
Orange Curaçao liqueur	3 tbsp.	50 mL
Whipping cream (or 1 envelope topping)	1 cup	250 mL

Crust: Melt butter in saucepan. Stir in graham crumbs and brown sugar.
Press in ungreased 8 inch (20 cm) springform pan. Chill.

Filling: Sprinkle gelatin over water in small saucepan. Let stand for 5 minutes. Heat and stir to dissolve.

Beat cream cheese and cottage cheese together in bowl until smooth. Beat in next 5 ingredients in order given. Add gelatin mixture and beat.

Whip cream until stiff. Fold into cheese mixture. Turn into prepared pan. Chill. Remove pan sides. Serves 8 to 12.

Pictured on this page.

CHERRY BANANA SLICE

A pretty fruited bavarian-type dessert. Luscious!

CRUST

Butter or hard margarine	½ **cup**	125 mL
Vanilla wafer crumbs	1½ **cups**	375 mL

FILLING

Raspberry-flavored gelatin (jelly powder)	1 × 3 oz.	1 × 85 g
Boiling water	1 cup	250 mL
Cherry pie filling	19 oz.	540 mL
Cream cheese, softened	4 oz.	125 g
Granulated sugar	⅓ cup	75 mL
Whipping cream (or 1 envelope topping)	1 cup	250 mL
Miniature marshmallows	1 cup	250 mL
Small bananas, sliced	2	2

Crust: Melt butter in saucepan. Stir in wafer crumbs. Reserve ½ cup (125 mL). Press remaining crumbs in ungreased 9 x 9 inch (22 x 22 cm) pan.

Filling: Dissolve gelatin in boiling water. Stir into pie filling. Chill until syrupy.

Beat cream cheese and sugar together until fluffy. Set aside.

Whip cream until stiff. Fold in marshmallows, bananas and cheese mixture. Fold into thickened gelatin. Turn into prepared crust. Scatter reserved crumbs over top. Chill. Serves 9.

Pictured on page 9.

TIP

Cut a piece of waxed paper to fit the bottom of a springform pan. Place in pan before starting recipe. Cheesecake will slide off the metal bottom onto serving plate much easier.

CHOCOLATE CHEESECAKE

This chilled cheesecake fills the craving for chocolate. It is creamy and has a lot of height to it. Decorate with whipped topping and raspberries.

CRUST

Hard margarine	2 tbsp.	30 mL
Chocolate wafer crumbs	⅔ cup	150 mL

FILLING

Envelopes dessert topping	2	2
Skim milk	1 cup	250 mL
Envelopes unflavored gelatin	2 × ¼ oz.	2 × 7 g
Water	½ cup	125 mL
Cocoa	½ cup	125 mL
Low-fat cream cheese (less than 20% MF), softened	8 oz.	250 g
Low-fat cottage cheese (less than 1% MF), smoothed in blender or sieved	1 cup	250 mL
Liquid sweetener	3 tbsp.	50 mL
Vanilla	1 tsp.	5 mL
Chocolate wafer crumbs	1 tbsp.	15 mL

Crust: Melt margarine in small saucepan. Stir in wafer crumbs. Press in bottom of 8 inch (20 cm) springform pan. Chill.

Filling: Combine dessert topping and milk according to package directions. Whip until stiff. Set aside.

Sprinkle gelatin over water in small saucepan. Let stand for 1 minute. Heat and stir to dissolve gelatin. Remove from heat.

Add cocoa. Whisk to blend. Cool to room temperature.

Beat cream cheese, cottage cheese, sweetener and vanilla together in medium bowl until smooth. Add cocoa mixture. Beat slowly to mix. Fold in whipped topping. Pour into prepared pan. Smooth top.

Sprinkle with wafer crumbs. Chill. Makes 12 servings.

Pictured on this page.

Chilled desserts are so convenient to make ahead and to have ready when company arrives. They are pretty-as-a-picture and yet so simple to make. Your guests will appreciate the extra effort you took to prepare such an exquisite dessert—but we know the truth!

DESSERT BLUES

Chilled or frozen, this is an attractive make-ahead.

CRUST

Butter or hard margarine, melted	1/2 cup	125 mL
Graham cracker crumbs	1 1/2 cups	375 mL
Granulated sugar	1/4 cup	60 mL
Chopped walnuts	1/2 cup	125 mL

FILLING

Large white marshmallows	8 oz.	250 g
Milk	1/2 cup	125 mL
Whipping cream (or 1 envelope topping)	1 cup	250 mL
Canned blueberry pie filling	19 oz.	540 mL
Granulated sugar	1/4 cup	60 mL
Lemon juice, fresh or bottled	2 tsp.	10 mL

Crust: Mix all 4 ingredients well. Reserve 1/2 cup (125 mL). Press remainder in 9 x 13 inch (22 x 33 cm) pan.

Filling: Heat marshmallows and milk together, stirring often, until melted. Cool to room temperature.

Whip cream in small bowl until stiff. Fold in marshmallow mixture. Spread over crumbs in pan. Chill for 1 hour.

Mix pie filling, sugar and lemon juice. Spoon over top. Sprinkle with reserved crumbs. Chill for several hours or overnight. Cuts into 12 pieces.

DANISH CREAM SQUARES

This creamy dessert will certainly spark conversation. Delightful to look at. Delightful to eat.

Whole graham crackers		
Vanilla pudding and pie filling, 6 serving size	**1**	**1**
Milk	**2½ cups**	**625 mL**
Whipping cream (or 1 envelope topping)	**1 cup**	**250 mL**
Granulated sugar	**1 tbsp.**	**15 mL**
Vanilla	**½ tsp.**	**2 mL**
Whole graham crackers		
Icing (confectioner's) sugar	**1½ cups**	**375 mL**
Milk	**3 tbsp.**	**50 mL**
Semisweet chocolate baking square	**1 × 1 oz.**	**1 × 28 g**
Butter or hard margarine	**1 tsp.**	**5 mL**

Line 9 x 13 inch (22 x 33 cm) ungreased pan with graham crackers, trimming to fit.

Cook pudding with milk as directed on package. Allow to cool. Spread over crackers in pan.

Whip cream, sugar and vanilla until stiff. Spread over pudding.

Place another layer of graham crackers over pudding, trimming to fit.

Mix icing sugar and milk well. Add more sugar or milk if needed to make a fairly runny glaze. Spread over cracker layer.

Melt chocolate with butter over hot water. Drizzle over top of icing. Chill. Let stand overnight before using. Cuts into 15 pieces.

Pictured on page 23.

Clockwise from top: Pink Lady, page 24;
Danish Cream Squares, page 22; and Chilled Dessert, page 25.

PINK LADY

Lots of flavors here. Raspberry, pineapple and strawberry combine to make this a winning dessert.

CRUST

Butter or hard margarine, melted	½ cup	125 mL
Graham cracker crumbs	2 cups	500 mL
Granulated sugar	⅓ cup	75 mL

FILLING

Reserved pineapple juice, plus water to make	1 cup	250 mL
Large marshmallows	16	16
Raspberry-flavored gelatin (jelly powder)	1 × 3 oz.	1 × 85 g
Boiling water	1 cup	250 mL
Cold water	1 cup	250 mL
Sliced fresh strawberries	1 cup	250 mL
Canned pineapple chunks, diced	14 oz.	398 mL
Whipping cream (or 1 envelope topping)	1 cup	250 mL
Slivered almonds	½ cup	125 mL
Vanilla	½ tsp.	2 mL

Coconut, sprinkle

Crust: Melt butter in saucepan. Stir in graham crumbs and sugar. Press ⅔ in ungreased 8 x 8 inch (20 x 20 cm) pan.

Filling: Put juice and marshmallows into top of double boiler. Heat over simmering water, stirring often, until melted.

Dissolve gelatin in boiling water. Add cold water. Stir into marshmallow mixture. Chill until syrupy.

Add strawberries and pineapple.

Whip cream until stiff. Fold in nuts and vanilla. Fold into thickened mixture. Pour ½ mixture over prepared crust. Sprinkle with remaining crumbs. Spoon second ½ cream mixture over top.

Sprinkle with coconut. Chill. Serves 9.

Pictured on page 23 and on page 80.

CHILLED DESSERT

A mild chocolate nutty filling on a wafer crust.

CRUST

Vanilla wafer crumbs	1¼ cups	300 mL
Butter or hard margarine, softened	¼ cup	60 mL

FILLING

Whipping cream (or 1 envelope topping)	1 cup	250 mL
Butter or hard margarine, softened	½ cup	125 mL
Milk	¼ cup	60 mL
Vanilla	1 tsp.	5 mL
Icing (confectioner's) sugar	2 cups	500 mL
Cocoa	3 tbsp.	50 mL
Chopped pecans or walnuts	¾ cup	175 mL

Crust: Mix graham crumbs and butter until crumbly. Press about ½ crumb mixture in ungreased 8 x 8 inch (20 x 20 cm) pan.

Filling: Whip cream in small bowl until stiff. Set aside.

Using same beaters combine butter, milk, vanilla, icing sugar and cocoa in separate bowl. Beat very slowly at first so milk won't spatter. Beat until light and fluffy.

Stir in nuts. Fold in whipped cream. Spread over crumb crust in pan. Sprinkle with remaining crumbs. Chill for several hours or overnight. Cuts into 9 pieces.

Pictured on page 23.

PARÉ
pointer

When a kitten

crawls into a

photocopier it

comes out a copycat.

LEMON JELLY DESSERT

A light dessert, sort of like a cheesecake without any cheese. Slight lemon flavor. Just right after a heavy meal.

CRUST
Graham cracker crumbs, good sprinkle

FILLING		
Lemon-flavored gelatin (jelly powder)	**1 × 3 oz.**	**1 × 85 g**
Boiling water	**1 cup**	**250 mL**
Cold water	**½ cup**	**125 mL**
Evaporated milk, freezer chilled	**14 oz.**	**385 mL**
Granulated sugar	**1 cup**	**250 mL**
Juice of 1 lemon		

Graham cracker crumbs, good sprinkle

Crust: Sprinkle crumbs to cover bottom of ungreased 9 x 9 inch (22 x 22 cm) pan, or if you would like more not-so-deep servings, use 19 x 3 inch (22 x 33 cm) pan.

Filling: Stir gelatin with boiling water to dissolve. Add cold water. Chill until syrupy.

Beat partially frozen milk until soft peaks form. Add sugar and lemon juice. Beat again until quite stiff. Beat in thickened gelatin. Carefully pour filling over crumbs. Smooth top.

Sprinkle crumbs over top. Chill. Serves 9 generously.

· PARÉ
pointer

Don't let your dog

eat garlic or his bark

really will be worse

than his bite.

APPLE CREAM DESSERT

Fresh apples over crumb crust with a creamy topping.

CRUST

Graham cracker crumbs	1¼ cups	300 mL
Granulated sugar	2 tbsp.	30 mL
Butter or hard margarine, melted	⅓ cup	75 mL

FILLING

Butter or hard margarine	1 tbsp.	15 mL
Medium apples, peeled, cored and sliced	5	5
Ground cinnamon, sprinkle		
Large eggs	3	3
Sour cream	1 cup	250 mL
Granulated sugar	½ cup	125 mL
Lemon juice, fresh or bottled	½ tsp.	2 mL
Vanilla	½ tsp.	2 mL
Salt	⅛ tsp.	0.5 mL

Crust: Mix graham crumbs, sugar and melted butter in small bowl. Measure and reserve 2 tbsp. (30 mL) for topping. Press remaining crumbs in ungreased 8 x 8 inch (20 x 20 cm) pan.

Filling: Melt butter in frying pan. Add apple and sauté for 2 minutes. Cover. Simmer slowly until soft. Sprinkle with cinnamon. Cool. Pour over crust.

Beat eggs in top of double boiler. Mix in sour cream, sugar, lemon juice, vanilla and salt. Cook, stirring often, until slightly thickened. Pour over apples. Sprinkle with reserved crumbs. Chill for at least 2 to 3 hours. Cuts into 9 pieces.

Pictured on this page.

Have you ever made cookies on the stove instead of in the oven? No-bake drop or ball cookies are perfect for any occasion. They are mouth-watering and eye-appealing when rolled in coconut, nuts or even dipped in a glaze. These all freeze well.

GINGER CHOCO COOKIES

These no-bake cookies are made from gingersnap crumbs. They are soft and creamy.

Semisweet chocolate chips	**2 cups**	**500 mL**
Sour cream	**½ cup**	**125 mL**
Lemon juice, fresh or bottled	**1 tsp.**	**5 mL**
Gingersnap crumbs	**2 cups**	**500 mL**
Icing (confectioner's) sugar	**1 cup**	**250 mL**

Melt chocolate chips in sour cream and lemon juice in heavy medium saucepan over low heat. Stir often to hasten melting. Be careful not to boil. Remove from heat.

Add cookie crumbs and icing sugar. Stir to moisten. Shape into 1 inch (2.5 cm) balls. These may be left as is, rolled in icing sugar or dipped in Chocolate Glaze, below. Makes about 4 dozen.

CHOCOLATE GLAZE: Mix 1 cup (250 mL) icing (confectioner's) sugar with 2 tbsp. (30 mL) cocoa. Add enough water to make a barely pourable glaze. Dip tops of cookie balls and let dry on tray.

Pictured on page 29.

ORANGE BALLS

These no-bake cookies have a real orange flavor. Freeze well.

Vanilla wafer crumbs	4 cups	1 L
Butter or hard margarine, softened	¹/₂ cup	125 mL
Icing (confectioner's) sugar	2¹/₂ cups	625 mL
Chopped pecans or walnuts	¹/₂ cup	125 mL
Frozen concentrated orange juice, thawed	6 oz.	170 g
Medium coconut or chocolate sprinkles	2 cups	500 mL

Combine first 5 ingredients in bowl. Mix well. Shape into 1 inch (2.5 cm) balls.

Roll in coconut. Makes 5 dozen.

Pictured on this page.

BOILED CHOCOLATE COOKIES

This is probably the most used recipe of young first-time cooks. No oven is required.

Butter or hard margarine	¹/₂ cup	125 mL
Milk	¹/₂ cup	125 mL
Granulated sugar	2 cups	500 mL
Cocoa	¹/₂ cup	125 mL
Rolled oats (not instant)	2¹/₂ cups	625 mL

Put butter, milk, sugar and cocoa into saucepan. Bring to a boil, stirring often. Boil for 5 minutes.

Remove from heat. Stir in rolled oats. Drop by teaspoonfuls onto waxed paper. Makes about 4 dozen.

Variation: To make these more special, add coconut, cherries and/or nuts.

Top: Ginger Choco Cookies, page 28. Bottom: Orange Balls, page 29.

Top: Creamy Snowballs.
Bottom: Chocolate Peanut Drops.

CREAMY SNOWBALLS

If you have a sweet tooth these are for you. Creamy.

Cream cheese, softened	4 oz.	125 g
Icing (confectioner's) sugar	2 cups	500 mL
Milk	2 tbsp.	30 mL
Semisweet chocolate chips, melted	⅔ cup	150 mL
Vanilla	½ tsp.	2 mL
Miniature colored marshmallows	3 cups	750 mL
Medium coconut		

Combine first 5 ingredients in bowl. Beat together until smooth.

Fold in marshmallows. Mix well. Chill for 30 minutes. Shape into 1½ inch (3 cm) balls.

Roll in coconut. These freeze well. Makes about 3½ dozen.

Pictured on this page.

CHOCOLATE PEANUT DROPS

Peanut butter adds to the flavor of these saucepan cookies.

Milk	½ cup	125 mL
Butter or hard margarine	½ cup	125 mL
Granulated sugar	2 cups	500mL
Cocoa	6 tbsp.	100 mL
Smooth peanut butter	¾ cup	175 mL
Vanilla	1 tsp.	5 mL
Rolled oats (not instant)	3 cups	750 mL
Chopped nuts (optional)	½ cup	125 mL

Put milk, butter, sugar and cocoa into medium saucepan. Heat and stir until boiling. Remove from heat.

Stir in peanut butter and vanilla. Add rolled oats and nuts. Mix. Drop by spoonfuls onto waxed paper. Makes about 4½ dozen.

Pictured on this page.

What better to have handy in the freezer than a delicious frozen dessert! If you only serve two or three pieces, freeze the rest for the next time. Have several in the freezer when planning a birthday party or a special get together. Everyone loves the cool refreshing taste of frozen desserts.

VANILLA ICE CREAM

À la mode your desserts. Practically cholesterol free. You will want to double or triple the recipe after you try it.

Skim evaporated milk	1 cup	250 mL
Corn starch	2 tsp.	10 mL
Granulated sugar	$\frac{1}{2}$ cup	125 mL
Salt, just a pinch		
Envelope dessert topping	1	1
Skim milk	$\frac{1}{2}$ cup	125 mL
Vanilla	2 tsp.	10 mL

Whisk first 4 ingredients together in small saucepan. Heat and stir until mixture boils and thickens. Cool to room temperature.

Whip dessert topping and skim milk together according to package directions until stiff. Beat in vanilla. Fold into milk mixture. Pour into shallow 8 x 8 inch (20 x 20 cm) pan. Freeze. Makes about 2$\frac{1}{4}$ cups (560 mL).

FROZEN HAWAIIAN PIE

Mashed banana is the subtle flavor in this pie. With a taste of Hawaii.

Miniature marshmallows	2 cups	500 mL
Canned crushed pineapple, with juice	14 oz.	398 mL
Grated lemon peel	¹/₂ tsp.	2 mL
Medium banana, mashed	1	1
Lemon juice, fresh or bottled	1¹/₂ tsp.	7 mL
Whipping cream (or 1 envelope topping)	1 cup	250 mL
Commercial graham cracker crust	1	1

Combine marshmallows, pineapple with juice and lemon peel in medium heavy saucepan. Place over medium-low heat. Stir often as marshmallows melt. Chill well, stirring occasionally, until thickened.

Stir in banana and lemon juice.

Whip cream in small bowl until stiff. Fold into pineapple-banana mixture.

Pour into crust. Freeze, uncovered. Cover and store in freezer. Remove from freezer and leave at room temperature for at least 30 minutes before cutting. Serves 8 to 10.

Pictured on this page.

Top: Frozen Mocha Cheesecake, page 36. Bottom: Watermelon Bombe, page 34.

WATERMELON BOMBE

An easy-to-make ice cream dessert. A green shell with pink "flesh".
The seeds are chocolate chips.

Pistachio ice cream or lime sherbet, softened	1 qt.	1 L
Strawberry ice cream, softened	1 qt.	1 L
Semisweet chocolate chips	½ cup	125 mL

Line melon mold or bowl with plastic wrap. Using back of spoon press pistachio ice cream to completely line inside of mold. Freeze for 10 minutes.

Stir strawberry ice cream and chocolate chips together. Fill center of mold. Return to freezer. Unmold a few minutes before serving. Cuts into 6 to 8 slices of the coldest watermelon ever.

Pictured on page 33.

LEMON FREEZE

A snap to make. Let the youngest cook make this.

Whipping cream	1½ cups	375 mL
Milk	½ cup	125 mL
Grated peel of 1 lemon		
Lemon juice, fresh or bottled	⅓ cup	75 mL
Granulated sugar	1 cup	250 mL

Measure all 5 ingredients into medium bowl. Stir to dissolve sugar. Place in freezer for 2 to 3 hours until frozen. Serves 6 to 8.

PARÉ
pointer

Jimmy's grades were

under water. His

teacher said they

were below C level.

CHOCO MINT PIE

Chocolate and mint are meant for each other. A frozen duo.

CHOCOLATE CRISP CRUST

Butter or hard margarine	**2 tbsp.**	**30 mL**
Semisweet chocolate chips	**²/₃ cup**	**150 mL**
Crisp rice cereal	**2 cups**	**500 mL**

FILLING

Crème de Menthe, (or 1 tsp., 5 mL **peppermint flavoring)**	**¹/₃ cup**	**75 mL**
Chocolate ice cream, softened	**1 qt.**	**1 L**
Chocolate Sauce, page 61		

Chocolate Crisp Crust: Melt butter and chocolate chips in medium saucepan over low heat. Stir often to hasten melting. Remove from heat. Add cereal. Stir to coat. Press on bottom and up sides of 9 inch (22 cm) pie plate. Freeze.

Filling: Stir Crème de Menthe into ice cream. Mix well. Spoon into chocolate crust. Freeze. Cover to store. Spoon Chocolate Sauce over each serving. Serves 8 to 10.

Pictured below.

FROZEN MOCHA CHEESECAKE

A worker's dream. Cut a piece or two and pop the rest back into the freezer.

CRUST

Butter or hard margarine	½ **cup**	**125 mL**
Graham cracker crumbs	1½ **cups**	**375 mL**
Granulated sugar	¼ **cup**	**60 mL**
Cocoa	¼ **cup**	**60 mL**

FILLING

Cream cheese, softened	**8 oz.**	**250 g**
Sweetened condensed milk	**11 oz.**	**300 mL**
Chocolate-flavored syrup	⅔ **cup**	**150 mL**
Instant coffee granules	**1 tbsp.**	**15 mL**
Hot water	**1 tsp.**	**5 mL**
Whipping cream (or 1 envelope topping)	**1 cup**	**250 mL**

Crust: Melt butter in medium saucepan over medium heat. Stir in graham crumbs, sugar and cocoa. Reserve ½ cup (125 mL). Press remaining crumbs in bottom and up sides of ungreased 9 inch (22 cm) springform pan.

Filling: Beat cream cheese until fluffy. Beat in condensed milk and chocolate syrup.

Dissolve coffee in hot water. Add to cheese mixture.

Whip cream until stiff. Fold into cheese mixture. Pour into prepared pan. Scatter reserved crumbs over top. Freeze. Serves 8.

Pictured on page 33.

DRUMSTICK CAKE

A fabulous dessert to keep on hand in the freezer.

FIRST LAYER

Butter or hard margarine	¼ cup	60 mL
Smooth peanut butter	3 tbsp.	50 mL
Chocolate wafer crumbs	1½ cups	375 mL
Finely chopped pecans	½ cup	125 mL

SECOND LAYER

Cream cheese, softened	8 oz.	250 g
Granulated sugar	½ cup	125 mL
Smooth peanut butter	½ cup	125 mL
Large eggs	2	2
Milk	2 tbsp.	30 mL
Vanilla	1½ tsp.	7 mL
Frozen whipped topping, thawed	4¼ cups	1 L

THIRD LAYER

Chocolate sundae topping	¼ cup	60 mL
Butterscotch sundae topping	¼ cup	60 mL
Reserved chocolate wafer crumb mixture	½ cup	125 mL

First Layer: Melt butter in medium saucepan. Stir in peanut butter. Add wafer crumbs and pecans. Mix. Reserve ½ cup (125 mL) for third layer. Press remaining crumb mixture in bottom of ungreased 9 x 13 inch (22 x 33 cm) pan.

Second Layer: Beat cream cheese, sugar and peanut butter together until smooth. Beat in eggs, 1 at a time. Add milk and vanilla. Mix.

Fold in topping. Spread over first layer.

Third Layer: Drizzle chocolate and butterscotch toppings over second layer or if you prefer, stir them together first, then drizzle over top. Sprinkle with reserved crumb mixture. Cover. Freeze overnight. Let stand for about 10 minutes at room temperature before serving. Serves 12 to 15.

Pictured on this page.

FROZEN CHOCOLATE PIE

Nutty with a whipped smooth texture.

FILLING

Cream cheese, softened	**8 oz.**	**250 g**
Granulated sugar	**1 cup**	**250 mL**
Salt	**¼ tsp.**	**1 mL**
Vanilla	**1 tsp.**	**5 mL**
Semisweet chocolate chips	**1 cup**	**250 mL**
Milk	**⅓ cup**	**75 mL**
Whipping cream (or 1 envelope topping)	**1 cup**	**250 mL**
Chopped pecans or walnuts	**½ cup**	**125 mL**
Commercial chocolate cookie crust	**1**	**1**

Filling: Combine first 4 ingredients in bowl. Beat until smooth.

Heat chocolate chips and milk together in small saucepan on low until melted. Stir often. Cool. Place saucepan in cold water to hasten cooling. Beat cooled chocolate mixture into cream cheese mixture.

Whip cream in small bowl until stiff. Fold in.

Add pecans and fold in.

Turn into cookie crust. Freeze. Serve plain or topped with whipped cream or Chocolate Sauce, page 61. Serves 8.

Pictured on page 39.

PARÉ
pointer

If you could only

combine old

automobiles with

nylons, you would

have cars that run.

Left: Frozen Chocolate Pie, page 38. Right: Frosty Clouds, page 39.

FROSTY CLOUDS

The name says it all. Everyone will want your "ice cream" recipe—but it isn't. Great freezer food.

Granulated sugar	½ **cup**	**125 mL**
Water	**3 tbsp.**	**50 mL**
Egg whites (large), room temperature	**2**	**2**
Whipping cream	½ **cup**	**125 mL**
Vanilla	½ **tsp.**	**2 mL**

Measure sugar and water into small saucepan. Cook and stir over medium heat until a thread forms when spoon is lifted. Remove from heat.

Beat egg whites until stiff. Slowly pour sugar-water mixture into whites while beating continuously until light-colored. Cool.

Whip cream and vanilla together until stiff. Fold into egg white mixture. Spoon into muffin tins lined with paper cups, rounding tops nicely. Freeze. Cover to store. To serve, unmold and add your favorite fruit. Makes 10 medium.

Pictured above.

The presentation of crêpes is magnificent as the finale of a special dinner. Try Chocolate Crêpes as a change from the usual. Mix and match the fruits, sauces and types of crêpe. All will disappear from dessert plates. Fruits are always a welcomed ending to a meal. They require little preparation and always look so sensational.

BANANA BUTTERSCOTCH

This has to be a must for an easy dessert. A delicious way to use bananas.

Brown sugar, packed	1 cup	250 mL
Butter or hard margarine	3 tbsp.	60 mL
Light cream	2 tbsp.	30 mL
Vanilla	$1/8$ tsp.	0.5 mL
Medium bananas, sliced	3	3
Whipping cream	$1/2$ cup	125 mL
Granulated sugar	1 tsp.	5 mL
Vanilla	$1/2$ tsp.	2 mL

Combine brown sugar, butter, cream and first amount of vanilla in saucepan. Bring to a boil. Simmer slowly to thicken slightly.

Slice bananas into 4 fruit nappies.

Whip cream, granulated sugar and second amount of vanilla until stiff. Spoon hot butterscotch topping over bananas and top with whipped cream. Serves 4.

STRAWBERRIES ROMANOFF

Definitely for fresh strawberries only. Quick, easy and very impressive.

Ripe medium strawberries	**1 qt.**	**1 L**
Icing (confectioner's) sugar	**½ cup**	**125 mL**
Prepared orange juice	**½ cup**	**125 mL**
Curaçao (or Grand Marnier or Cointreau)	**1 tsp.**	**5 mL**
Whipping cream	**1 cup**	**250 mL**
Granulated sugar	**1 tbsp.**	**15 mL**
Curaçao (or Grand Marnier or Cointreau)	**1 tsp.**	**5 mL**

Combine strawberries, icing sugar, orange juice and first amount of Curaçao in bowl. Chill, covered, for several hours, turning or stirring occasionally. Divide fruit and juice among 8 champagne glasses, sherbets or other containers.

Whip cream and granulated sugar together until stiff. Add second amount of Curaçao for flavoring. Spoon over berries. Serves 8.

Variation: Granulated sugar may be substituted for the icing sugar.

APRICOTS ROMANOFF: Substitute fresh apricots for strawberries.

Pictured on front cover.

PEACHES ROMANOFF: Substitute fresh peaches for strawberries.

BLUEBERRIES ROMANOFF: Substitute fresh blueberries for strawberries.

TIP

Choose the freshest and least-bruised fruit to use in these recipes. When fruits are heated, they will soften. If they are already overripe or bruised, they will become mushy.

CRÊPES

So many variations can be made from basic crêpes. They freeze so well.

Large eggs	**4**	**4**
Milk	**1 cup**	**250 mL**
Water	**1 cup**	**250 mL**
All-purpose flour	**2 cups**	**500 mL**
Cooking oil	**¼ cup**	**60 mL**
Granulated sugar	**1 tsp.**	**5 mL**
Salt	**¼ tsp.**	**1 mL**

Beat eggs together in large bowl until frothy. Add remaining 6 ingredients. Beat until smooth. Cover and store in refrigerator overnight or for at least a few hours. Add milk before cooking if too thick. Pour 2 tbsp. (30 mL) in greased hot crêpe pan. Tip pan to swirl batter all over pan bottom. Remove when underside is lightly browned. Stack with waxed paper between each crêpe. Secure in plastic bag to store in freezer. Use as needed. Makes 24 crêpes.

CHOCOLATE CRÊPES: Take out 2 tbsp. (30 mL) flour and add 2 tbsp. (30 mL) cocoa. Used in Black Forest Crêpes recipe, pictured on page 43.

CHOCOLATE-SAUCED CRÊPES: Cut vanilla (or strawberry or chocolate) ice cream in 1 x 1 x 4 inch (2.5 x 2.5 x 10 cm) long pieces and lay on edge of unbrowned side of crêpe. Roll. Allow 2 crêpes per serving. Spoon hot Chocolate Sauce, page 61, over top.

STRAWBERRY-SAUCED CRÊPES: Roll and fill as for Chocolate-Sauced Crêpes. Spoon warm Strawberry Sauce, page 59, over top.

BLUEBERRY-SAUCED CRÊPES: Roll and fill as for Chocolate-Sauced Crêpes. Spoon warm Blueberry Sauce, page 60, over top.

BUTTERSCOTCH-SAUCED CRÊPES: Roll and fill as for Chocolate-Sauced Crêpes. Spoon warm Butterscotch Sauce, page 59, over top.

Sauced crêpes above, pictured on page 5 and on page 47.

APRICOT CRÊPES: Roll and fill as for Chocolate-Sauced Crêpes. Spoon warm Apricot Sauce, page 61, over top.

PARÉ *pointer*

If you stand for

nothing, you will fall

for something.

BLACK FOREST CRÊPES

Just a few minutes and your dessert is ready. Having a supply of crêpes in the freezer really helps.

Prepared Chocolate Crêpes, page 42	16	16
Kirsch or sherry (optional)	⅓ cup	75 mL
Canned cherry pie filling (cold or hot)	19 oz.	540 mL
Granulated sugar	¼ cup	60 mL
Ground nutmeg	⅛ tsp.	0.5 mL
Sweetened whipped cream		
Chocolate curls for garnish		

Sprinkle crêpes with kirsch or sherry.

Mix cherry pie filling, sugar and nutmeg in small bowl. Spoon about 2 tbsp. (30 mL) close to 1 side of crêpe. Roll. Allow 2 per serving. Lay on plate.

Spoon whipped cream over top. Garnish with chocolate curls. Serves 8.

Pictured on this page.

STRAWBERRY CREAM CRÊPES

Crêpes spread with a cream cheese mixture and topped with strawberries.

Cream cheese, softened	8 oz.	250 g
Granulated sugar	¼ cup	60 mL
Sour cream	1 cup	250 mL
Prepared Crêpes, page 42	12	12
Sliced fresh strawberries	2 cups	500 mL
Granulated sugar	¼ cup	60 mL

Beat cream cheese, first amount of sugar and sour cream together well.

Spread cheese mixture over unbrowned sides of crêpes. Roll.

Stir strawberries and sugar together. Spoon over crêpes. Allow 2 per serving. Serves 6.

CRISPY FRUIT PIZZA

A dessert pizza you can eat with your fingers. Can be made the day before. THIS IS AWESOME! Do not freeze.

CRUST		
Butter or hard margarine	¼ cup	60 mL
Large marshmallows	32	32
Crisp rice cereal	5 cups	1.25 L
TOPPING		
Cream cheese, softened	8 oz.	250 g
Icing (confectioner's) sugar	2 cups	500 mL
Cocoa	¼ cup	60 mL
Small strawberries, halved, reserve 1 whole berry	16	16
Banana, peeled and sliced	1	1
Kiwifruit, peeled, halved lengthwise and sliced	2	2
GLAZE		
Apricot jam	2 tbsp.	30 mL
Water	1½ tsp.	7 mL
Whipping cream (or 1 envelope topping)	1 cup	250 mL
Granulated sugar	2 tsp.	10 mL
Vanilla	½ tsp.	2 mL

Crust: Combine butter and marshmallows in saucepan. Stir often on medium-low until melted.

Remove saucepan from heat. Add rice cereal. Stir until well coated. Grease 12 inch (30 cm) pizza pan. Press cereal mixture evenly in pan with wet fingers. Cool in refrigerator.

(continued on next page)

Topping: Place cream cheese, icing sugar and cocoa in small bowl. Beat on low until moistened. Beat on medium until smooth. Spread over cooled pizza base.

Arrange strawberries, banana and kiwifruit over chocolate topping in fancy design.

Glaze: Mix jam and water in small cup. With pastry brush, dab fruit with jam mixture to glaze and to prevent fruit from turning brown.

Whip cream, sugar and vanilla together in medium bowl until stiff. Put dabs on top of pizza. Cuts into 8 or 10 wedges.

Pictured below.

FRIED APPLES

A quick frying pan dessert. Can easily be increased.

Medium size cooking apples (such as Golden Delicious or McIntosh)	4	4
Lemon juice, fresh or bottled	2 tsp.	10 mL
Butter or hard margarine	2 tbsp.	30 mL
Brown sugar, packed	2 tbsp.	30 mL
Butter or hard margarine	1 tbsp.	15 mL
Graham cracker crumbs	¼ cup	60 mL
Granulated sugar	1 tsp.	5 mL

Peel apples. Quarter and cut each quarter into 3 slices. Combine with lemon juice in large bowl. Toss well to coat.

Melt first amount of butter in large frying pan. Add brown sugar. Add apple and cover. Cook for about 15 minutes until apples are tender, stirring occasionally. Divide among 4 bowls.

Melt second amount of butter in small saucepan. Stir in graham crumbs and granulated sugar. Sprinkle over apple. Serves 4.

PARÉ
pointer

If you have

something round

with a bad temper,

you have a vicious

circle.

Clockwise from top: Blueberry-Sauced Crêpes, page 42; Chocolate-Sauced Crêpes, page 42; Strawberry-Sauced Crêpes, page 42; Butterscotch-Sauced Crêpes, page 42; Chilled Blueberry Pie, page 49; and Cherry Pine Pie, page 50.

PEACH MELBA

What color! An easy dessert, well received.

MELBA SAUCE

Frozen sweetened raspberries in heavy syrup, thawed	10 oz.	284 g
Cornstarch	1 tbsp.	15 mL
Water	2 tbsp.	30 mL
Scoops vanilla ice cream	4	4
Sweetened sliced peaches, canned, fresh or frozen	20	20

Melba Sauce: Drain and heat raspberry syrup in small saucepan over medium heat until it boils.

Stir cornstarch into water then into boiling syrup until mixture boils and thickens. Remove from heat. Mash raspberries and add to thickened syrup. Stir to cool.

Put scoop of ice cream into each sherbet or fruit nappy. Surround with 5 peach slices. Top with Melba Sauce. Serves 4.

RUMMY MELON

You probably never will find so light or so refreshing a dessert as this. A good hot day picker-upper!

Water	¼ cup	60 mL
Lemon juice, fresh or bottled	1 tbsp.	15 mL
Lime juice, fresh or bottled	1 tbsp.	15 mL
Rum flavoring	1 tsp.	5 mL
Liquid sweetener	1 tbsp.	15 mL
Cubed watermelon (or pineapple)	5 cups	1.25 L

Stir first 5 ingredients together in small bowl.

Put watermelon into medium bowl. Drizzle juice over top. Toss to coat. Chill for about 3 hours. Stir fruit 2 or 3 times during chilling. Makes 4 servings.

P A R É
pointer

No wonder time flies

so fast, so many

people are trying to

kill it.

All of these pies are made with commercial graham or chocolate crumb crusts. This makes it not only no-bake but also quick and convenient. This is a great excuse to get out of making fussy pastry. The fillings are made either on the stove or in the microwave.

CHILLED BLUEBERRY PIE

You'll argue over who gets the last piece.

Cream cheese, softened	**8 oz.**	**250 g**
Icing (confectioner's) sugar	**1 cup**	**250 mL**
Lemon juice, fresh or bottled	**1 tbsp.**	**15 mL**
Frozen whipped topping, thawed	**2 cups**	**500 mL**
Commercial graham cracker crust	**1**	**1**
Canned blueberry pie filling	**19 oz.**	**540 mL**

Beat cream cheese, icing sugar and lemon juice in small bowl until smooth.

Fold whipped topping into cheese mixture.

Pour into graham crust. Chill for about 2 hours.

Spoon pie filling over top. You probably will not need to use the whole can, but lots of topping is always acceptable. Chill. Serves 8.

Pictured on page 47.

CHERRY PINE PIE

The perky flavor comes from the raspberry gelatin. Walnuts add a touch of crunch. Makes two pies.

Canned crushed pineapple, with juice	**19 oz.**	**540 mL**
Cornstarch	**1 tbsp.**	**15 mL**
Raspberry-flavored gelatin (jelly powder)	**1 × 3 oz.**	**1 × 85 g**
Canned cherry pie filling	**19 oz.**	**540 mL**
Granulated sugar	**¾ cup**	**175 mL**
Almond flavoring	**¼ tsp.**	**1 mL**
Chopped walnuts	**¾ cup**	**175 mL**
Commercial graham cracker crusts	**2**	**2**
Whipping cream (or 2 envelopes topping)	**2 cups**	**500 mL**
Granulated sugar	**4 tsp.**	**20 mL**
Vanilla	**1 tsp.**	**5 mL**

Combine pineapple with juice, cornstarch and raspberry gelatin in saucepan. Heat and stir until mixture boils and thickens. Remove from heat.

Add pie filling, first amount of sugar almond flavoring and walnuts. Stir.

Pour into graham crusts. Chill.

Whip cream, second amount of sugar and vanilla together until stiff. Spoon onto each pie. Serves 16.

Pictured on page 47.

PARÉ
pointer

When young Harvie was asked to use the words "defeat", "defence" and "detail" in a sentence he replied, "Defeat went over defence before detail".

LIME CHIFFON PIE

Especially welcome on a summer day, this is good in a pastry crust but is extra special in a chocolate crust.

Envelope unflavored gelatin	1 x ¼ oz.	1 x 7 g
Water	¼ cup	60 mL
Lime juice, fresh or bottled	½ cup	125 mL
Egg yolks (large)	4	4
Granulated sugar	⅔ cup	150 mL
Finely grated lime peel	1 tsp.	5 mL
Egg whites (large), room temperature	4	4
Granulated sugar	½ cup	125 mL
Whipping cream (or 1½ envelopes topping)	1½ cups	375 mL
Drops of green food coloring (optional)	2-4	2-4
Commercial chocolate cookie crust	1	1
Chocolate curls		
Reserved whipped cream	1 cup	250 mL

Sprinkle gelatin over water in heavy saucepan. Let stand for 1 minute. Heat and stir until mixture boils.

Combine next 4 ingredients in small bowl. Beat well with spoon. Stir into boiling gelatin until mixture returns to a boil. Cool then chill until mixture mounds when dropped from spoon.

Beat egg whites until a stiff froth. Gradually beat in second amount of sugar until stiff and sugar is dissolved. Fold into thickened mixture.

Whip cream in small bowl until stiff. Reserve 1 cup (250 mL). Fold remaining cream into gelatin mixture. Fold in green food coloring if using. Pour into chocolate cookie crust. Chill.

To serve, place a cluster of chocolate curls in center. Pipe border of reserved whipped cream around outside edge. Chill. Serves 8.

Pictured on front cover.

DAIQUIRI PIE: Use only 2 tbsp. (30 mL) water instead of ¼ cup (60 mL). Add 2 to 3 tbsp. (30 to 50 mL) of light rum to water. Go by taste.

BRANDY ALEXANDER PIE

A classic that has always been with us. Very light.

Envelope unflavored gelatin	1 x ¼ oz.	1 x 7 g
Water	½ cup	125 mL
Granulated sugar	⅔ cup	150 mL
Egg yolks (large)	3	3
Crème de Cacao	2 tbsp.	30 mL
Brandy	2 tbsp.	30 mL
Egg whites (large), room temperature	3	3
Whipping cream (or 1 envelope topping)	1 cup	250 mL
Commercial graham cracker crust	1	1
Whipping cream (or 1 envelope topping)	1 cup	250 mL
Icing (confectioner's) sugar	1 tbsp.	15 mL

Sprinkle gelatin over water in small saucepan. Let stand for 1 minute. Heat and stir to dissolve gelatin.

Mix sugar and egg yolks in small bowl. Add to gelatin and stir until mixture starts to boil. Remove from heat.

Add Crème de Cacao and brandy. Chill until mixture mounds slightly when spooned over itself.

Beat egg whites in small bowl until stiff. Fold into chilled filling.

Using same beaters and bowl, whip first amount of cream until stiff. Fold into filling. Turn into graham crust. Chill.

Whip second amount of cream and icing sugar until stiff. Spoon onto pie. Serves 8.

Pictured on this page.

BANANA CREAM PIE

Sliced banana in a cream filling topped with whipped cream. Delicious.

FILLING

Granulated sugar	¹/₂ cup	125 mL
Cornstarch	3 tbsp.	50 mL
Large egg	1	1
Vanilla	¹/₂ tsp.	2 mL
Milk	2 cups	500 mL
Salt	¹/₂ tsp.	2 mL
Bananas, sliced	2	2
Commercial graham cracker crust	1	1

TOPPING

Whipped cream (or 1 envelope topping)	1 cup	250 mL
Granulated sugar	2 tsp.	10 mL
Vanilla	¹/₂ tsp.	2 mL

Filling: Stir sugar and cornstarch together well in large bowl. Mix in egg, vanilla, milk and salt. Microwave, uncovered, on high (100%) power for about 6 minutes stirring at half time, until mixture boils and thickens. Cool for about 30 minutes.

Stir in bananas. Pour into graham crust. Chill.

Topping: Whip cream, sugar and vanilla together until stiff. Spread over chilled pie. Chill for at least 2 hours before serving. Serves 8.

TIP

Keep a stock of the pre-made commercial graham crumb crusts and chocolate cookie crumb crusts in your freezer. They come in so handy when unexpected company gives you 24 hours—or less—notice of their arrival! Quickly prepare one of these recipes, store in the refrigerator and voilà —dessert!

Rich and creamy puddings are always appreciated. Whether served hot or cold, puddings can always warm the spirit. Covering the pudding with waxed paper touching the top will eliminate the skin that forms over the top as it cools.

CREAMY CHOCOLATE PUDDING

Wonderful flavor to this old-fashioned pudding. Best eaten fresh.

Granulated sugar	1¼ cups	300 mL
All-purpose flour	½ cup	125 mL
Cocoa	½ cup	125 mL
Salt	½ tsp.	2 mL
Milk	3 cups	750 mL
Butter or hard margarine	2 tbsp.	30 mL
Large egg	1	1
Vanilla	2 tsp.	10 mL

Mix sugar, flour, cocoa and salt in medium saucepan. Stir well. Gradually add milk, stirring to mix. Add butter. Stir over medium until pudding boils and thickens.

Beat egg and vanilla together in small bowl until smooth. Add 2 or 3 spoonfuls of hot pudding to egg mixture. Stir. Pour into pudding in saucepan, stirring, until mixture returns to a boil. Boil 1 minute. Serve hot, or place plastic wrap on surface of pudding and cool on counter. After it has cooled, refrigerate until well chilled. Makes 4 cups (1 L).

BLUEBERRY GRUNT

It is said of this old recipe that it made a grunting sound as it cooked, thus the name.

Blueberries, fresh or frozen	5 cups	1.25 L
Granulated sugar	1 cup	250 mL
Water	½ cup	125 mL
Lemon juice, fresh or bottled	1 tsp.	5 mL
TOPPING		
All-purpose flour	2 cups	500 mL
Granulated sugar	¼ cup	60 mL
Baking powder	2 tsp.	10 mL
Salt	½ tsp.	2 mL
Butter or hard margarine	2 tbsp.	30 mL
Milk	1 cup	250 mL

Combine blueberries, sugar, water and lemon juice in large saucepan. Heat until boiling. Simmer gently while preparing topping.

Topping: Measure flour, sugar, baking powder and salt into bowl. Stir to mix. Cut in butter.

Add milk. Mix until moistened. Drop by spoonfuls onto simmering berries. Simmer, covered, for 15 minutes without peeking. Serve warm with cream or ice cream. Serves 8.

Pictured below.

CHOCOLATE CREAM PUDDING

An easy, from-the-shelf dessert.

Envelope dessert topping	1	1
Milk	½ cup	125 mL
Semisweet chocolate chips, melted and cooled	⅓ cup	75 mL
Instant chocolate pudding powder, 4 serving size	1	1
Milk	2 cups	500 mL
Chocolate shavings, for garnish		

Combine dessert topping, first amount of milk and melted chocolate chips in small bowl. Beat until stiff. Reserve ¼ cup (60 mL) for topping.

Add pudding powder and second amount of milk. Mix. Beat on high for 2 minutes. Pour into sherbets or fruit nappies. Top with dab of reserved topping. Garnish with chocolate shavings. Serves 4 to 6.

Pictured on this page.

STRAWBERRY BUTTERSCOTCH

An unlikely combination. A pretty dishful. A light, tasty dessert.

Butterscotch or caramel pudding and pie filling, 6 serving size, cooked as package directs	1	1
Frozen strawberries, with syrup	1 cup	250 mL
Whipping cream (or 1 envelope topping)	1 cup	250 mL
Granulated sugar	1 tbsp.	15 mL
Vanilla	½ tsp.	2 mL

Spoon cooked and chilled pudding into 6 sherbets or fruit nappies. Spoon strawberries over top.

Whip cream, sugar and vanilla together until stiff. Put a dollop on top of each. Serves 6.

RICE PUDDING

This just might be the best rice pudding you will ever eat.

Long grain rice	1 cup	250 mL
Water	2 cups	500 mL
Cinnamon stick (about 4 inches, 10 cm)	1	1
Milk	4 cups	1 L
Granulated sugar	1 cup	250 mL
Raisins	½ cup	125 mL
Salt	¼ tsp.	1 mL
Egg yolks (large)	3	3
Vanilla	1 tsp.	5 mL

Combine rice, water and cinnamon stick in medium saucepan. Cover and bring to a boil. Simmer for about 15 minutes until rice is cooked and water is absorbed. Remove cinnamon stick.

Heat milk in heavy saucepan. Stir in sugar, raisins and salt. Add rice. Simmer slowly, uncovered, for about 15 minutes until thick but still soft, stirring often.

Beat egg yolks in small bowl. Stir in vanilla. Add about ½ cup (125 mL) hot rice to egg yolk mixture. Stir all back into hot rice. Cook and stir for about 1 minute. Ready to serve 8 people, ¾ cup (175 mL) each.

PARÉ
pointer

The teacher would

only have six pupils

in her schoolroom.

She wanted her area

to have a little class.

MINUTE TAPIOCA PUDDING

A frothy milk pudding with a butterscotch flavor. Anything but ordinary.
A family favorite.

Egg yolk (large)	1	1
Milk	2 cups	500 mL
Brown sugar, packed	1/3 cup	75 mL
Butter or hard margarine	1/4 cup	60 mL
Minute tapioca	3 tbsp.	50 mL
Salt	1/8 tsp.	0.5 mL
Egg white (large), room temperature	1	1
Brown sugar, packed	2 tbsp.	30 mL
Vanilla	1/2 tsp.	2 mL

Put egg yolk into heavy saucepan. Stir in small amount of milk until smooth, then stir in rest of milk followed by next 4 ingredients. Heat and stir over medium until mixture comes to a full rolling boil. Remove from heat. It will seem too runny but will thicken on standing.

Beat egg white in medium bowl until soft peaks form. Add half of brown sugar at a time continuing to beat until stiff. Add vanilla. Pour hot tapioca-milk mixture slowly into beaten egg white, folding as you pour. Serve warm. Leftovers may be eaten cold. Serves 6.

REGULAR MINUTE TAPIOCA: Use granulated sugar instead of brown sugar. A few chopped nuts may be added.

CHOCOLATE MINUTE TAPIOCA: Add 3 tbsp. (50 mL) chocolate drink powder to first ingredients.

PARÉ
pointer

Not knowing what

he might fall against

on his way off the

ladder, he fell

against his will.

The smoothness and richness of these easy sauces make dessert worth craving. Choose any of these sauces to complement the dessert you are making tonight. Whether it is cake, ice cream, crêpes or simply a plate of fruit, these sauces will enhance the appearance—not to mention the taste!

BUTTERSCOTCH SAUCE

An easy make-your-own sauce. Serve with Butterscotch-Sauced Crêpes, page 42.

Light cream	1 cup	250 mL
Brown sugar, packed	1 cup	250 mL
Corn syrup, light or dark	1 cup	250 mL
Butter or hard margarine	1/3 cup	75 mL
Vanilla	1 tsp.	5 mL
Salt	1/8 tsp.	0.5 mL

Measure all 6 ingredients into saucepan. Heat and stir over medium until mixture boils. Boil and stir for 2 minutes. Cool. Makes 2 1/2 cups (625 mL).

Pictured on page 47.

STRAWBERRY SAUCE

So easy and so versatile. Spoon over ice cream, cake, or serve with Strawberry-Sauced Crêpes, page 42.

Frozen strawberries in syrup, drained, syrup reserved	15 oz.	425 g
Cornstarch	1 tbsp.	15 mL

Put reserved syrup into small saucepan. Stir in cornstarch. Bring to a boil, stirring, until thickened. Cool. Stir in strawberries. Makes about 2 cups (500 mL).

Pictured on page 47.

RASPBERRY COULIS

Try koo-LEE for a picture-perfect dessert. Serve with Chocolate Paté, page 71.

Frozen raspberries in syrup, thawed	15 oz.	425 g
Reserved syrup, plus water to make	1¼ cups	300 mL
Granulated sugar	2 tbsp.	30 mL
Cornstarch	4 tsp.	20 mL

Strain raspberries through sieve. Reserve syrup.

Pour reserved syrup plus water mixture into saucepan.

Mix in sugar and cornstarch. Heat and stir until mixture boils and thickens. Cool. Pour onto plate before or after dessert is placed on plate. Makes 1¼ cups (300 mL).

Pictured on page 71.

BLUEBERRY SAUCE

If you want a filling from scratch, this is an excellent way to get that good fresh taste.

Blueberries, fresh or frozen	10 oz.	284 g
Water	½ cup	125 mL
Granulated sugar	½ cup	125 mL
Cornstarch	1 tbsp.	15 mL
Lemon juice, fresh or bottled	1 tbsp.	15 mL

Combine all 5 ingredients in saucepan. Stir well. Heat and stir over medium until boiling. Simmer gently for about 5 minutes until berries release their juice. Serve with Blueberry-Sauced Crêpes, page 42, or waffles. Makes a scant 2 cups (500 mL).

Pictured on page 47.

CHOCOLATE SAUCE

Spoon over scoops of ice cream or Chocolate-Sauced Crêpes, page 42.

Unsweetened chocolate baking squares, cut up	**2 × 1 oz.**	**2 × 28 g**
Granulated sugar	**¹/₂ cup**	**125 mL**
Skim evaporated milk	**1 cup**	**250 mL**
Vanilla	**¹/₂ tsp.**	**2 mL**

Put all 4 ingredients into saucepan. Heat on medium, stirring often, until melted and simmering. Reduce heat. Simmer, whisking constantly for about 20 minutes until smooth and thickened. Makes 1 cup (250 mL).

Pictured on page 47.

APRICOT SAUCE

A good combination of flavors. Tangy.

Apricot jam	**1 cup**	**250 mL**
Prepared orange juice	**2 tbsp.**	**30 mL**
Brandy flavoring	**¹/₂ tsp.**	**2 mL**

Mix all 3 ingredients well. Serve warm with Apricot Crêpes, page 42, or cold over ice cream or cake. Makes 1 cup (250 mL).

PARÉ
pointer

Maybe oranges don't

think but we all

know how they

concentrate.

It is always so convenient to have a supply of squares in the freezer just waiting for company to arrive. These no-bake squares are easy and fun to prepare. Enjoy the richness of each morsel.

TV ROLL

Try this differently colored marshmallow roll.

Large egg, beaten	1	1
Brown sugar, packed	1 cup	250 mL
Graham cracker crumbs	½ cup	125 mL
Butter or hard margarine, melted	2 tbsp.	30 mL
Miniature colored marshmallows	2 cups	500 mL
Chopped walnuts	½ cup	125 mL
Colored thread coconut (see Note)		

Mix first 6 ingredients in order given. Squish and mix by hand. Work between waxed paper or dip hands in cold water as you work to shape into log.

Roll log in coconut. Wrap in waxed paper, folding in ends to hold shape. Chill overnight or freeze. Cuts into thin slices as needed.

Note: If you cannot buy colored thread coconut, put desired food coloring drops in container with lid. Add coconut. Shake or stir to distribute color.

Pictured on front cover.

MIDNIGHT MINTS

The perfect ending to lunch or supper. The minty taste goes with just about anything.

BOTTOM LAYER

Butter or hard margarine	½ cup	125 mL
Granulated sugar	¼ cup	60 mL
Cocoa	⅓ cup	75 mL
Large egg, fork beaten	1	1
Graham cracker crumbs	1¾ cups	425 mL
Finely chopped walnuts	½ cup	125 mL
Fine coconut	¾ cup	175 mL

SECOND LAYER

Butter or hard margarine, softened	⅓ cup	75 mL
Milk	3 tbsp.	50 mL
Peppermint flavoring	1 tsp.	5 mL
Icing (confectioner's) sugar	2 cups	500 mL
Green food coloring		

TOP LAYER

Semisweet chocolate chips (see Note)	⅔ cup	150 mL
Butter or hard margarine	2 tbsp.	30 mL

Bottom Layer: Combine butter, sugar and cocoa in saucepan. Bring slowly to a boil. Stir in egg to thicken. Remove from heat.

Stir in graham crumbs, walnuts and coconut. Work together well. Press very firmly in greased 9 x 9 inch (22 x 22 cm) pan.

Second Layer: Combine butter, milk, flavoring and icing sugar in bowl. Beat together well adding a bit more milk if needed to make spreadable. Tint a pretty green. Spread over first layer.

Top Layer: Melt chocolate chips and butter together in saucepan over low heat or hot water. Stir often. Cool. When cool but still runny, spread over second layer. Chill and store, covered, in refrigerator or freezer. Cuts into 36 squares.

Note: You may also use 4 x 1 oz. (4 x 28 g) semisweet chocolate baking squares.

PARÉ
pointer

Gossip travels like a breeze when it is started by a couple of wind-bags.

SAUCEPAN BROWNIES

At last, a brownie that you can make on a day which is too hot to think about food. It has an exceptionally rich chocolate flavor.

Semisweet chocolate chips	2²/₃ cups	650 mL
Evaporated milk	1 cup	250 mL
Vanilla wafer crumbs	3 cups	750 mL
Miniature marshmallows	2 cups	500 mL
Chopped walnuts	1 cup	250 mL
Icing (confectioner's) sugar	1 cup	250 mL
Salt	¹/₂ tsp.	2 mL
Evaporated milk	2 tsp.	10 mL
Reserved chocolate mixture	¹/₂ cup	125 mL

Put chocolate chips and first amount of evaporated milk into large saucepan. Melt over medium-low heat, stirring often, until smooth. Remove from heat. Measure out ¹/₂ cup (125 mL) and reserve for final step.

Stir wafer crumbs, marshmallows, walnuts, icing sugar and salt into remaining chocolate mixture in saucepan. Mix well. Press in greased or foil-lined 9 x 9 inch (22 x 22 cm) pan.

Stir second amount of evaporated milk into the reserved chocolate mixture. Spread evenly over brownies. Chill. Cuts into 36 squares.

PARÉ
pointer

With a tire and

some musicians you

could have a rubber

band.

MARS BARS SQUARES

Candy bars with crisp cereal. Crisp and chocolaty.

Mars candy bars, cut up (black and red label)	**4 × 1¾ oz.**	**4 × 50 g**
Butter or hard margarine	**½ cup**	**125 mL**
Crisp rice cereal	**3 cups**	**750 mL**
TOPPING		
Semisweet chocolate chips	**1 cup**	**250 mL**
Butter or hard margarine	**¼ cup**	**60 mL**

Heat candy bars and butter together in large saucepan, stirring often, until melted. Remove from heat.

Add rice cereal. Stir to coat all cereal. Press in greased or foil-lined 9 × 9 inch (22 × 22 cm) pan.

Topping: Combine chocolate chips and butter in small saucepan over low, stirring often until smooth. Spread over all. Cool. Cuts into 36 squares.

Pictured below.

CHERRY CHOCOLATE SQUARES

An exquisite no-bake square. It has a chocolate base and top, with a cherry center. So pretty. So special.

BOTTOM LAYER

Butter or hard margarine	½ cup	125 mL
Granulated sugar	¼ cup	60 mL
Cocoa	⅓ cup	75 mL
Large egg, fork beaten	1	1
Graham cracker crumbs	1¾ cups	425 mL
Coconut	½ cup	125 mL
Finely chopped walnuts	⅓ cup	75 mL
Water	1 tbsp.	15 mL

SECOND LAYER

Butter or hard margarine, softened	¼ cup	60 mL
Maraschino cherry juice	2 tbsp.	30 mL
Almond flavoring	1 tsp.	5 mL
Icing (confectioner's) sugar	2 cups	500 mL
Chopped maraschino cherries	⅓ cup	75 mL

THIRD LAYER

Butter or hard margarine	2 tbsp.	30 mL
Semisweet chocolate chips	⅓ cup	75 mL

Bottom Layer: Put butter, sugar and cocoa into heavy saucepan over medium heat. Stir together to melt. Stir in egg and cook until thickened slightly. Remove from heat. Stir in crumbs, coconut, walnuts and water. Press very firmly in ungreased 9 x 9 inch (22 x 22 cm) pan.

Second Layer: Beat butter, cherry juice, almond flavoring and icing sugar together well. Beat slowly at first to keep sugar from flying all over. Blot cherries with paper towels. Stir in cherries. Drop dabs here and there over first layer then spread. Let stand for about 10 minutes. Using your hand, pat smooth.

Third Layer: Melt butter in small saucepan. Add chocolate chips and stir to melt. Pour over top of second layer and smooth with back of teaspoon. Work quickly so as not to bring any second layer up to the top. Chill. Cuts into 36 squares.

Pictured on front cover.

PEANUT SQUARES

This chocolaty goodie is a snap to make. Freezes well.

FIRST LAYER

Smooth peanut butter	1 cup	250 mL
Semisweet chocolate chips	1 cup	250 mL
Butterscotch chips	1 cup	250 mL

SECOND LAYER

Butter or hard margarine	1/2 cup	125 mL
Vanilla custard powder	2 tbsp.	30 mL
Evaporated milk	1/4 cup	60 mL
Icing (confectioner's) sugar	3 cups	750 mL
Maple flavoring	1/2 tsp.	2 mL

THIRD LAYER

Peanuts	1 cup	250 mL

First Layer: Combine peanut butter and all chips in saucepan. Heat over low, stirring often, until smooth. Spread 1/2 mixture in ungreased 9 x 13 inch (22 x 33 cm) pan. Chill until firm. Reserve second 1/2 mixture for third layer.

Second Layer: Measure butter, custard powder and milk into saucepan. Heat and stir together until mixture reaches a full rolling boil. Remove from heat. Add icing sugar and flavoring. Stir until mixture forms a ball. Cool to room temperature. Using spoon and your hand, press in smooth layer over firm chocolate base.

Third Layer: Add peanuts to reserved mixture. Stir and spread over second layer. Chill. Cuts into 54 squares.

Pictured on front cover.

TIP

Line pan with foil so that the square will be easier to remove. If you are going to cut it immediately, pull the foil away from the edges. If you are going to freeze it for a later time, bring the foil over the edges and add another piece of foil over the top. Rewrap entirely in one more layer of foil and freeze.

These fluffy whipped desserts are perfect after a heavy meal. Most of these recipes require chilling before serving. You can make them in the morning and have them ready and waiting. A dollop of whipped topping adds the finishing touch. These whipped desserts are not suitable for freezing.

APRICOT CHIFFON

Delicate and frothy.

Canned apricots, with juice, run through blender or press through sieve	14 oz.	398 mL
Granulated sugar	1/3 cup	75 mL
All-purpose flour	2 tbsp.	30 mL
Egg yolks (large)	2	2
Water	3 tbsp.	50 mL
Lemon juice, fresh or bottled	2 tsp.	10 mL
Vanilla	1/2 tsp.	2 mL
Egg whites (large), room temperature	2	2

Bring apricot purée to a boil over medium heat.

Mix next 6 ingredients in bowl. Stir into boiling purée until mixture returns to a boil and thickens. Remove from heat.

Beat egg whites until stiff. Fold into hot mixture. Turn into serving bowl or spoon directly into sherbets. Chill. Pass pouring cream on the side. Serves 4.

Pictured on page 69.

Clockwise from top left: Apricot Chiffon, page 68; Strawberry Bavarian, page 72; and Mint Dessert, page 74.

WHITE CHOCOLATE MOUSSE

Delectable. Best eaten fresh.

Granulated sugar	²/₃ cup	150 mL
Water	¹/₄ cup	60 mL
White chocolate chips	1 cup	250 mL
Whipping cream	1 cup	250 mL
Vanilla	1 tsp.	5 mL

Stir sugar and water together in saucepan over medium until hot and sugar is dissolved.

Add chocolate chips. Stir until melted and smooth. Cool saucepan in cold water in sink. Chill in refrigerator until cold. Whisk smooth.

Beat cream and vanilla together until stiff. Fold into chocolate mixture. Pour into serving dishes. Serves 6.

Pictured on this page.

CHOCOLATE MOUSSE

Tastes just like a diet wrecker. Dress it up with a dab of whipped topping if desired.

Skim milk powder	1¹/₂ cups	375 mL
Warm water	6 tbsp.	100 mL
Liquid sweetener	¹/₂ tsp.	2 mL
Instant chocolate pudding powder, 4 serving size	1	1
Cold water	1 cup	250 mL
Envelope dessert topping	1	1
Skim milk	¹/₂ cup	125 mL
Vanilla	¹/₂ tsp.	2 mL

Measure first 3 ingredients into blender. Process until smooth and thick.

Add pudding and cold water. Process until smooth. Turn into bowl.

Whip dessert topping, skim milk and vanilla in small bowl until stiff according to package directions. Fold into chocolate mixture. Makes 4 cups (1 L).

CHOCOLATE PATÉ

Most impressive. Can be prepared two days ahead. Do not freeze.

Butter or hard margarine	**1 cup**	**250 mL**
Semisweet chocolate chips	**3 cups**	**750 mL**
Instant coffee granules, rolled to a powder (optional)	**1 tsp.**	**5 mL**
Granulated sugar	**¹/₂ cup**	**125 mL**
Large eggs	**2**	**2**
Vanilla	**1 tsp.**	**5 mL**
Whipping cream (or 1 envelope topping)	**1¹/₂ cups**	**375 mL**
Raspberry Coulis, page 60		
White chocolate baking squares, melted	**2 × 1 oz.**	**2 × 28 g**

Line 9 x 5 x 3 inch (22 x 12 x 7 cm) loaf pan with plastic wrap. Melt butter in large saucepan on low. Add chocolate chips and coffee granules. Stir often until smooth. Pour into large bowl.

Add sugar. Beat together well. Add eggs, 1 at a time, while continuing to beat. Mix in vanilla.

Whip cream in small bowl until stiff. Fold into chocolate mixture. Turn into prepared pan. Cover loosely and chill all day or overnight in refrigerator. Unmold onto platter. Cut slices ³/₄ to 1 inch (2 to 2.5 cm) thick with hot knife and lay sideways on serving plate. Spoon Raspberry Coulis on one side or all around slice. Drizzle with melted white chocolate and make feathered design. Serves 10 to 12.

Pictured on this page.

STRAWBERRY BAVARIAN

A quick dessert for a hot summer day or anytime.

Strawberry-flavored gelatin	1 × 3 oz.	1 × 85 g
Boiling water	1 cup	250 mL
Frozen sliced strawberries with syrup, partly thawed	15 oz.	425 g
Whipping cream (or 1 envelope topping)	1 cup	250 mL

Dissolve gelatin in boiling water.

Add strawberries. Stir until mixed. Chill until syrupy.

Whip cream until stiff. Fold into thickened mixture. Pour into pretty bowl or over 9 x 9 inch (22 x 22 cm) crumb crust in pan. Chill. Serves 9.

Pictured on page 69.

MAPLE BAVARIAN

A smooth dessert, this is one of the best ways to use maple syrup.

Envelope unflavored gelatin	1 × 1/4 oz.	1 × 7 g
Water	1/2 cup	125 mL
Maple syrup	1 cup	250 mL
Large eggs	3	3
Salt	1/4 tsp.	1 mL
Milk	1/2 cup	125 mL
Whipping cream (or 1 envelope topping)	1 cup	250 mL

Sprinkle gelatin over water in top of double boiler. Let stand 5 minutes. Place over simmering water. Stir to dissolve.

Add maple syrup. Mix in eggs thoroughly, 1 at a time. Stir in salt and milk. Cook and stir until mixture coats metal spoon. Remove from heat. Chill until mixture begins to thicken. Stir occasionally.

Whip cream until stiff. Fold into egg mixture. Pour into mold or pretty bowl. Serve with extra whipped cream if desired. Serves 8.

PARÉ
pointer

Never be kind to a

termite. They will

eat you out of house

and home.

SPANISH CREAM

This old recipe fills the bill for a light touch after a heavy meal. A white dessert to show off a sauce of our choice.

Milk	**3 cups**	**750 mL**
Envelope unflavored gelatin	**1 x ¼ oz.**	**1 x 7 g**
Granulated sugar	½ cup	125 mL
Salt	¼ tsp.	1 mL
Egg yolks (large)	3	3
Vanilla	1 tsp.	5 mL
Egg whites (large), room temperature	**3**	**3**

Measure milk into top of double boiler. Sprinkle gelatin over top. Let stand for 5 minutes. Heat over simmering water.

Add sugar and salt. Mix a little of the hot mixture into egg yolks, then pour yolks and vanilla into double boiler. Cook and stir until mixture coats a metal spoon. This will take about 15 minutes. Remove from heat. Chill until mixture thickens enough to pile softly when spooned from one side to the other.

Beat egg whites until stiff. Fold into thickened mixture. Pour into pretty bowl or mold. Chill. Serve with whipped cream. Serves 8.

CHOCOLATE SPANISH CREAM: Add 1½ x 1 oz. (1½ x 28 g) unsweetened chocolate baking squares to milk in double boiler.

Pictured on this page.

MINT DESSERT

A cool, minty, melt-in-your-mouth finale. Showy with chocolate crumb base.

CRUST		
Butter or hard margarine	½ cup	125 mL
Graham cracker crumbs	2 cups	500 mL
Granulated sugar	¼ cup	60 mL
Cocoa	¼ cup	60 mL
FILLING		
Milk	1 cup	250 mL
Package of white marshmallows	8 oz.	250 g
Whipping cream (or 2 envelopes topping)	2 cups	500 mL
Crème de Menthe, green	½ cup	125 mL

Crust: Melt butter in saucepan. Stir in graham crumbs, sugar and cocoa. Press ⅔ crumb mixture in ungreased 9 x 13 inch (22 x 33 cm) pan. Chill.

Filling: Put milk and marshmallows in large saucepan over low heat to melt. Stir often. Allow to cool.

Whip cream until stiff. Add Crème de Menthe. Fold into cooled marshmallow mixture. Pour over crumb crust. Scatter remaining ⅓ crumb mixture over top. Chill. Cuts into 15 pieces.

Pictured on page 69.

PARÉ
pointer

If a physician has

laryngitis would he

be a hoarse doctor?

COFFEE CARAMEL

A light dessert fit for any company. Almonds give an added touch.
A convenient make-ahead.

Water	½ cup	125 mL
Envelope unflavored gelatin	1 × ¼ oz.	1 × 7 g
Granulated sugar	¼ cup	60 mL
Slivered almonds	¼ cup	60 mL
Instant coffee granules	1 tsp.	5 mL
Whipping cream (or ½ envelope topping)	½ cup	125 mL

Measure water in cup. Sprinkle gelatin over top. Let stand for 5 minutes.

Put sugar in heavy saucepan over medium heat. Melt, stirring, until a rich golden-brown. Add water-gelatin mixture, stirring well to dissolve. It will sputter at first but will settle down and dissolve as you stir.

Add almonds and coffee granules. Remove from heat. Chill until syrupy, stirring occasionally.

Whip cream until stiff. Fold into sugar-gelatin mixture. Turn into pretty bowl. Chill. Serves 6.

Pictured below.

BLACK FOREST SOUFFLÉ

A chocolate dessert as light as a feather.

Canned cherries, dark or sour, pitted, drained	14 oz.	398 mL
Envelopes unflavored gelatin	2 x ¼ oz.	2 x 7 g
Granulated sugar	½ cup	125 mL
Egg yolks (large)	3	3
Milk	2 cups	500 mL
Semisweet chocolate chips	⅔ cup	150 mL
Vanilla	1½ tsp.	7 mL
Brandy flavoring	½ tsp.	2 mL
Egg whites (large), room temperature	3	3
Whipping cream (or 2 envelopes topping)	2 cups	500 mL

Set a few cherries aside to be used as a garnish. Cut remaining cherries into quarters.

Stir gelatin and sugar together in medium saucepan. Mix in egg yolks and milk. Heat over low for about 5 minutes until gelatin is dissolved and eggs are cooked.

Add chocolate chips, vanilla and brandy flavoring. Stir to melt chips. Chill until syrupy, stirring occasionally.

Beat egg whites until stiff. Using same beaters, beat cream until stiff. Fold egg whites into gelatin mixture, then fold in cream. Fold in cut up cherries. Pour into 4 cup (1 L) soufflé dish with 3 inch (7.5 cm) waxed paper collar fastened around it. Chill. Remove collar. Garnish with cherries and shaved or grated chocolate. Cover side edge with crushed nuts if desired. Serves 8.

Pictured on front cover.

·PARÉ
pointer

To err is human.

To put the blame

on someone is even

more human.

Measurement Tables

Throughout this book measurements are given in Conventional and Metric measure. To compensate for differences between the two measurements due to rounding, a full metric measure is not always used. The cup used is the standard 8 fluid ounce. Temperature is given in degrees Fahrenheit and Celsius. Baking pan measurements are in inches and centimetres as well as quarts and litres. An exact metric conversion is given below as well as the working equivalent (Standard Measure).

OVEN TEMPERATURES

Fahrenheit (°F)	Celsius (°C)
175°	80°
200°	95°
225°	110°
250°	120°
275°	140°
300°	150°
325°	160°
350°	175°
375°	190°
400°	205°
425°	220°
450°	230°
475°	240°
500°	260°

SPOONS

Conventional Measure	Metric Exact Conversion Millilitre (mL)	Metric Standard Measure Millilitre (mL)
1/8 teaspoon (tsp.)	0.6 mL	0.5 mL
1/4 teaspoon (tsp.)	1.2 mL	1 mL
1/2 teaspoon (tsp.)	2.4 mL	2 mL
1 teaspoon (tsp.)	4.7 mL	5 mL
2 teaspoons (tsp.)	9.4 mL	10 mL
1 tablespoon (tbsp.)	14.2 mL	15 mL

CUPS

1/4 cup (4 tbsp.)	56.8 mL	60 mL
1/3 cup (5 1/3 tbsp.)	75.6 mL	75 mL
1/2 cup (8 tbsp.)	113.7 mL	125 mL
2/3 cup (10 2/3 tbsp.)	151.2 mL	150 mL
3/4 cup (12 tbsp.)	170.5 mL	175 mL
1 cup (16 tbsp.)	227.3 mL	250 mL
4 1/2 cups	1022.9 mL	1000 mL (1 L)

PANS

Conventional Inches	Metric Centimetres
8x8 inch	20x20 cm
9x9 inch	22x22 cm
9x13 inch	22x33 cm
10x15 inch	25x38 cm
11x17 inch	28x43 cm
8x2 inch round	20x5 cm
9x2 inch round	22x5 cm
10x4 1/2 inch tube	25x11 cm
8x4x3 inch loaf	20x10x7 cm
9x5x3 inch loaf	22x12x7 cm

DRY MEASUREMENTS

Conventional Measure Ounces (oz.)	Metric Exact Conversion Grams (g)	Metric Standard Measure Grams (g)
1 oz.	28.3 g	30 g
2 oz.	56.7 g	55 g
3 oz.	85.0 g	85 g
4 oz.	113.4 g	125 g
5 oz.	141.7 g	140 g
6 oz.	170.1 g	170 g
7 oz.	198.4 g	200 g
8 oz.	226.8 g	250 g
16 oz.	453.6 g	500 g
32 oz.	907.2 g	1000 g (1 kg)

CASSEROLES (CANADA & BRITAIN)

Standard Size Casserole	Exact Metric Measure
1 qt. (5 cups)	1.13 L
1 1/2 qts. (7 1/2 cups)	1.69 L
2 qts. (10 cups)	2.25 L
2 1/2 qts. (12 1/2 cups)	2.81 L
3 qts. (15 cups)	3.38 L
4 qts. (20 cups)	4.5 L
5 qts. (25 cups)	5.63 L

CASSEROLES (UNITED STATES)

Standard Size Casserole	Exact Metric Measure
1 qt. (4 cups)	900 mL
1 1/2 qts. (6 cups)	1.35 L
2 qts. (8 cups)	1.8 L
2 1/2 qts. (10 cups)	2.25 L
3 qts. (12 cups)	2.7 L
4 qts. (16 cups)	3.6 L
5 qts. (20 cups)	4.5 L

Index

COOKBOOKS

Pink Lady, page 24.

Company's Coming cookbooks are available at retail locations everywhere.

For information contact:

COMPANY'S COMING PUBLISHING LIMITED

Box 8037, Station "F"   Box 17870
Edmonton, Alberta   San Diego, California
Canada T6H 4N9   U.S.A. 92177-7870

TEL: (403) 450-6223
FAX: (403) 450-1857